GUITAR • VOCAL WITH TABLATURE

THE ACOUSTIC GUITAR
SAMPLER

ISBN 1-57560-147-8

Visit our website at www.cherrylane.com

P9-AFB-571

Blackbird

Words and Music by
John Lennon and Paul McCartney

*Strum upstemmed notes w/index fin. of pick hand whenever more than one upstemmed note appears.

3

4

Cat's in the Cradle

Words and Music by
Harry Chapin and Sandy Chapin

Moderately, with a 2 feel

*A5

Let ring

*Strum with index finger.

sim.

A   C

My   child   ar - rived___   just   the   oth - er   day;   he
son   turned ten ___   just   the   oth - er   day;   He said,

D   A

came   to   the   world   in   the   u - su - al   way.___   But there were planes   to   catch___   and
"Thanks   for   the   ball,   Dad, come   on,   let's   play.___   Can you teach me   to   throw?"   I   said,

*To play along with recording, place capo at 8th fret.

bills to pay.__ He learned to walk while I was a-way. And he was
Not to-day.__ I got a lot to do." He said, "That's o-kay." And he,

talk-in' 'fore I knew it. And as he grew he'd say, "I'm gon-na be like
he walked a-way but his smile nev-er dimmed, it said "I'm gon-na be like

you, Dad. You know I'm gon-na be like you."
him, yeah. You know I'm gon-na be like him."   And the

cat's in the cra-dle and the sil-ver spoon,__ lit-tle boy blue and the man__

in the moon.

1.2. "When you com-in' home, Dad?" "I don't know when, but
3.4. "When you com-in' home, Son?" "I don't know when,

3rd time to Coda I;
4th time to Coda II;

we'll get to-geth-er then.____
we'll get to-geth-er then, _

You know we'll have a good time then."

My

Well, he came from col-lege just the oth-er day, so

much like a man I just had to say,__ "Son, I'm proud of you.__ Can you sit for a while?"__ He

shook his head and he said__ with a smile,__ "What I'd real - ly like, Dad, is to

bor - row the car keys. See ya lat - er, can I have them, please?"_____ And the

Dad.__ You know we'll have a good time then." *Instrumental* _____

Strum chords shown in TAB

I've
long since re-tired, my son's moved a-way. I called him up just the oth-er day. I said, "I'd
like to see— you if you don't mind.. He said, "I'd love to, Dad,— if I can find the time. You see, my
new job's a has-sle and the kids have the flu,— but it's sure nice talk-in' to you, Dad. It's been

Change the World

featured on the Motion Picture Soundtrack PHENOMENON

Words and Music by Gordon Kennedy,
Tommy Sims and Wayne Kirkpatrick

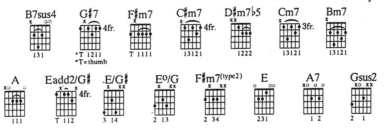

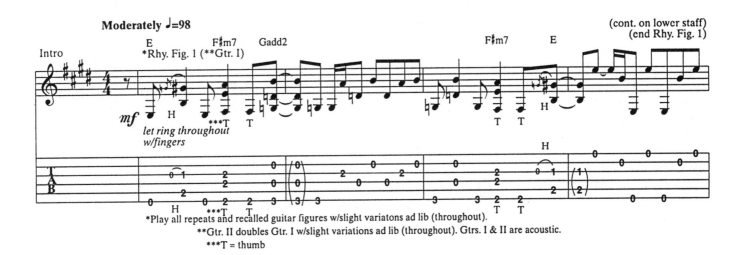

*Play all repeats and recalled guitar figures w/slight variatons ad lib (throughout).

**Gtr. II doubles Gtr. I w/slight variations ad lib (throughout). Gtrs. I & II are acoustic.

***T = thumb

*Clean tone w/chorus

**Vol. knob swell

Copyright © 1996 PolyGram International Publishing, Inc., Careers-BMG Music Publishing, Inc.,
MCA Music Publishing, A Division of Universal Studios, Inc., Bases Loaded Music and Sierra Skye Songs
Bases Loaded Music partially admin. by EMI Christian Music Publishing
International Copyright Secured   All Rights Reserved

*Rhy. Fig. 2 applies to Gtr. I only.

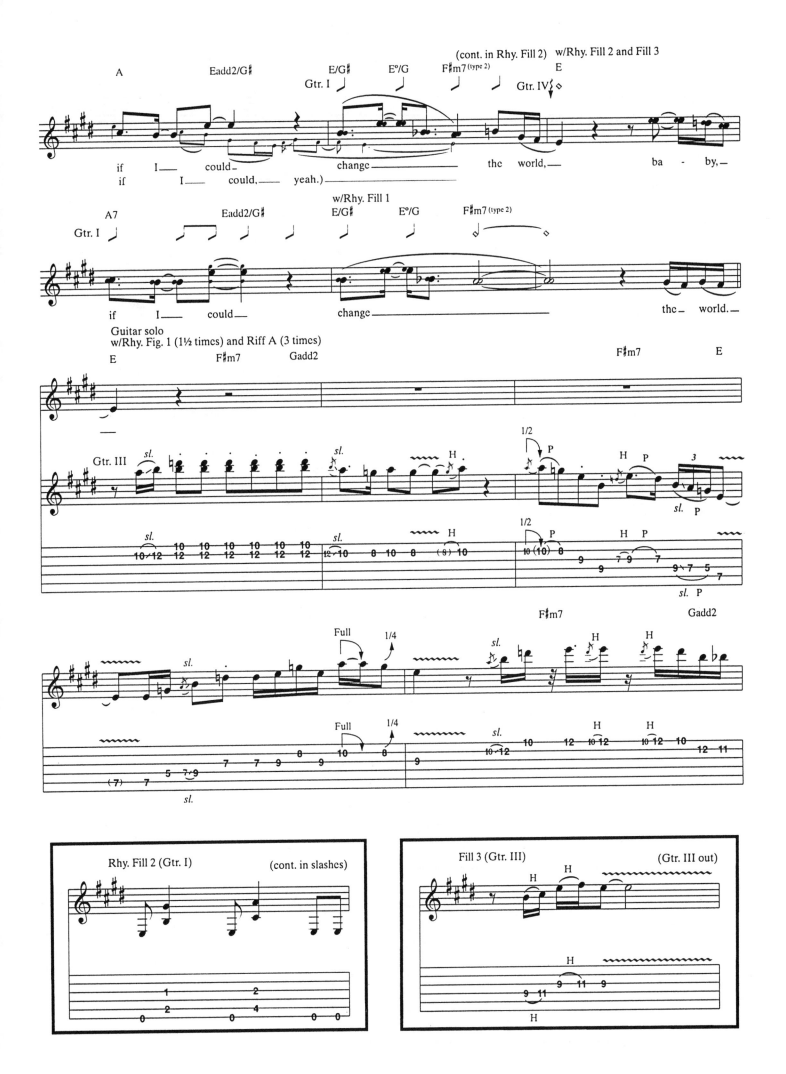

Crash into Me

Words and Music by
David J. Matthews

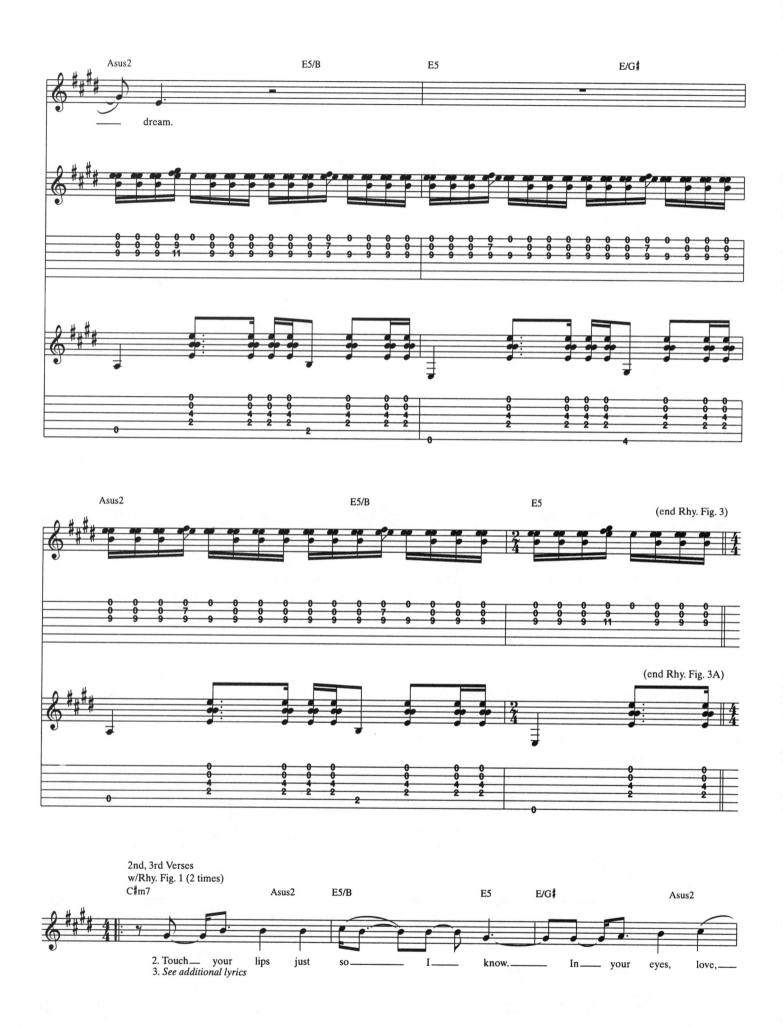

it glows___ so.___ I'm___ bare - boned___ and cra - zy for

you.___ Oh,___ when you___ come crash in - to me,

yeah, ba - by. And I come in - to___

you.___ In a boy's___

dream, in a boy's___ dream.

Oh,___ hike up your skirt a lit - tle more___ and show the___

_in - to me._ Crash _in - to me._

_Oh._ You know,_

I'm the king of the cas - tle, you're the dirt - y ras - cal. Crash in - to me._

Please, crash a lit - tle, babe._

No, no,_ no, oh, yes,_ I see the wave_ come and crash in - to me.

See the wave_ come and_ crash in - to me._ Crash_ in - to me.

w/vocal ad lib (till end)
w/Rhy. Fig. 1 (last 2 bars only) (Gtr. II)
w/Rhy. Fill 1
Repeat and fade

Additional Lyrics

3. Only if I've gone overboard,
   Then I'm begging you
   To forgive me, oh,
   In my haste.
   When I'm holding you so, girl,
   Close to me.
   Oh, and you come... *(To Chorus)*

Dee

Music by Randy Rhoads

Dust in the Wind

Words and Music by
Kerry Livgren

*Fingerpicking: m = middle; i = index; t = thumb (use thumb
for all downstemmed notes).
**Doubled by 12 stg. gtr.

3rd Verse
w/Rhy. Fig. 2

don't hang on, _____ noth-ing lasts for-ev-er but the earth_ and sky. It

slips a way, _____ and all your mon-ey won't an-oth-er min-ute buy. _____

Dust _____ in the wind. All we are_ is dust in_ the wind._

All we are_ is dust in_ the wind._____ Dust _____ in_ the wind. Ev-'ry-thing_ is dust in_ the

Ev-'ry-thing_ is dust in the wind.
wind. The _____ wind._

w/Ad lib vocal

Play 3 times and fade

Fire and Rain

Words and Music by
James Taylor

I Can't Help But Wonder

(Where I'm Bound)

Words and Music by
Tom Paxton

Additional Lyrics

2. I have wandered through this land just a-doin' the best I can,
   Tryin' to find what I was meant to do.
   And the people that I see look as worried as can be
   And it looks like they are wonderin' too. *(To Chorus)*

3. Oh, I had a little girl one time, she had lips like sherry wine
   And she loved me till my head went plumb insane.
   But I was too blind to see she was driftin' away from me
   And my good gal went off on the morning train. *(To Chorus)*

4. And I had a buddy back home but he started out to roam
   And I hear he's out by 'Frisco Bay.
   And sometimes when I've had a few, his old voice comes singin' through
   And I'm goin' out to see him some old day. *(To Chorus)*

5. If you see me passing by and you sit and you wonder why,
   And you wish that you were a rambler too;
   Nail your shoes to the kitchen door, lace 'em up and bar the door,
   Thank your stars for the roof that's over you. *(To Chorus)*

Little Martha

Words and Music by
Duane Allman

40

*Slowly pick strings from bottom to top.

Modoc

Music by Steve Morse

44

Patience

Words and Music by W. Axl Rose, Slash,
Izzy Stradlin', Duff McKagan
and Steven Adler

50

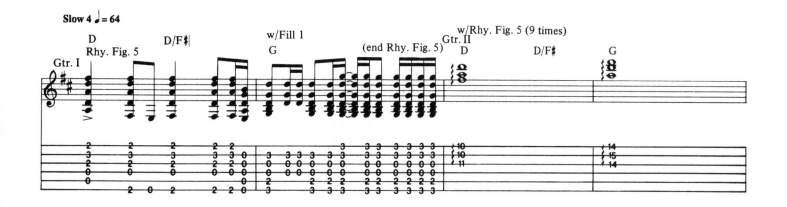

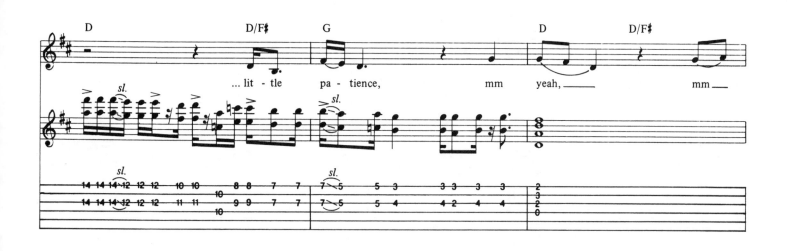

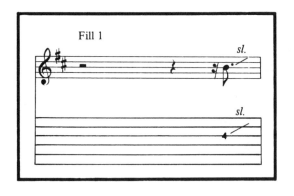

Additional Lyrics

2. I sit here on the stairs 'cause I'd rather be alone.
  If I can't have you right now I'll wait, dear.
  Sometimes I get so tense but I can't speed up the time.
  But you know, love, there's one more thing to consider.

  Said, woman, take it slow and things will be just fine.
  You and I'll just use a little patience.
  Said, sugar, take the time 'cause the lights are shining bright.
  You and I've got what it takes to make it.
  We won't fake it, ah, I'll never break it 'cause I can't take it. *(To Gtr. solo)*

Take Me Home, Country Roads

Words and Music by John Denver,
Bill Danoff and Taffy Nivert

55

Wild World

Words and Music by
Cat Stevens

*Gtr. I is piano arr. for gtr. Gtr. II is two acous. gtrs. arr. for one.
Gtr. II plays all parts w/slight strumming variations ad lib when repeated or recalled (throughout).

**All P.M.'s are slight (throughout).

***T = thumb

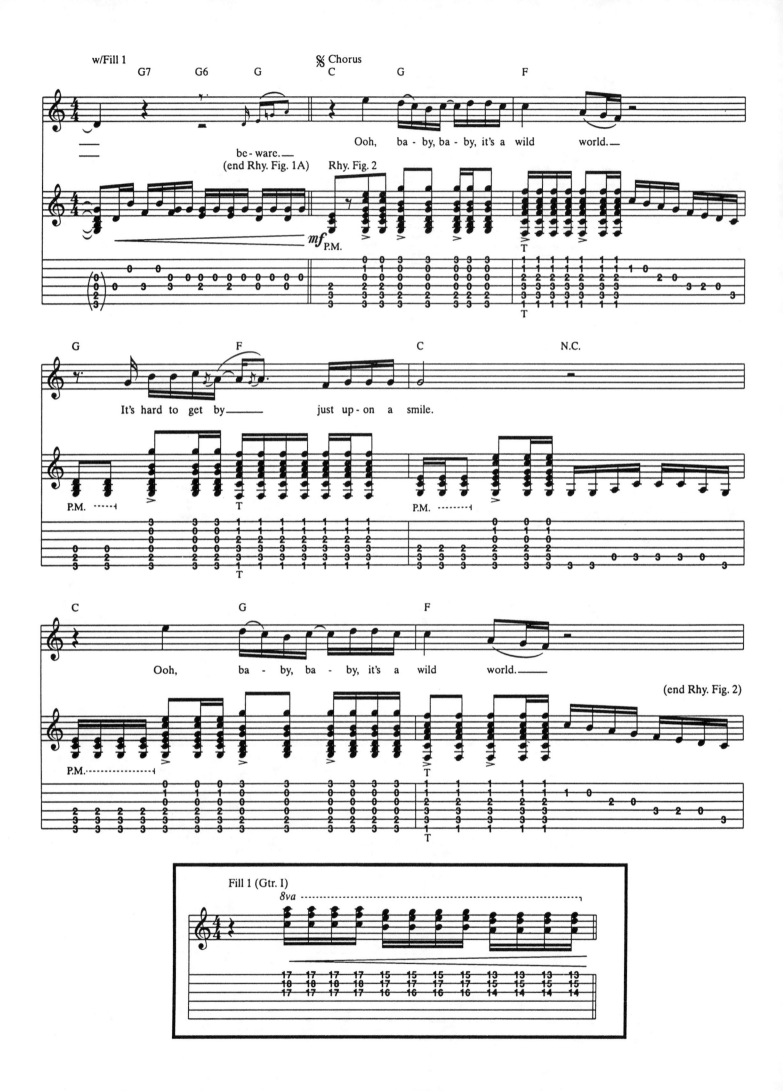

• *Tablature Explanation/Notation Legend* •

TABLATURE: A six-line staff that graphically represents the guitar fingerboard. By placing a number on the appropriate line, the string and the fret of any note can be indicated. For example:

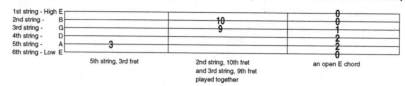

1st string - High E
2nd string - B
3rd string - G
4th string - D
5th string - A
6th string - Low E

5th string, 3rd fret   2nd string, 10th fret and 3rd string, 9th fret played together   an open E chord

Definitions for Special Guitar Notation

BEND: Strike the note and bend up a half step (one fret).

BEND: Strike the note and bend up a whole step (two frets).

BEND AND RELEASE: Strike the note and bend up a half (or whole) step, then release the bend back to the original note. All three notes are tied; only the first note is struck.

PRE-BEND: Bend the note up a half (or whole) step, then strike it.

PRE-BEND AND RELEASE: Bend the note up a half (or whole) step, strike it and release the bend back to the original note.

UNISON BEND: Strike the two notes simultaneously and bend the lower note to the pitch of the higher.

VIBRATO: Vibrate the note by rapidly bending and releasing the string with a left-hand finger.

WIDE OR EXAGGERATED VIBRATO: Vibrate the pitch to a greater degree with a left-hand finger or the tremolo bar.

SLIDE: Strike the first note and then with the same left-hand finger move up the string to the second note. The second note is not struck.

SLIDE: Same as above, except the second note is struck.

SLIDE: Slide up to the note indicated from a few frets below.

HAMMER-ON: Strike the first (lower) note, then sound the higher note with another finger by fretting it without picking.

PULL-OFF: Place both fingers on the notes to be sounded. Strike the first (higher) note, then sound the lower note by pulling the finger off the higher note while keeping the lower note fretted.

TRILL: Very rapidly alternate between the note indicated and the small note shown in parentheses by hammering on and pulling off.

TAPPING: Hammer ("tap") the fret indicated with the right-hand index or middle finger and pull off to the note fretted by the left hand.

NATURAL HARMONIC: With a left-hand finger, lightly touch the string over the fret indicated, then strike it. A chime-like sound is produced.

ARTIFICIAL HARMONIC: Fret the note normally and sound the harmonic by adding the right-hand thumb edge or index finger tip to the normal pick attack.

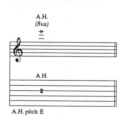

A.H. pitch: E

TREMOLO BAR: Drop the note by the number of steps indicated, then return to original pitch.

PALM MUTE: With the right hand, partially mute the note by lightly touching the string just before the bridge.

MUFFLED STRINGS: Lay the left hand across the strings without depressing them to the fretboard; strike the strings with the right hand, producing a percussive sound.

PICK SLIDE: Rub the pick edge down the length of the string to produce a scratchy sound.

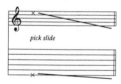

pick slide

TREMOLO PICKING: Pick the note as rapidly and continuously as possible.

trem. pick

RHYTHM SLASHES: Strum chords in rhythm indicated. Use chord voicings found in the fingering diagrams at the top of the first page of the transcription.

SINGLE-NOTE RHYTHM SLASHES: The circled number above the note name indicates which string to play. When successive notes are played on the same string, only the fret numbers are given.